The True Story of Jadav Payeng

THE BOY WHO GREW A FOREST

By Sophia Gholz ✦ Illustrated by Kayla Harren

PUBLISHED BY SLEEPING BEAR PRESS

The best time to plant a tree was twenty years ago.
The second best time to plant a tree is now.
—proverb

In India,
on a large river island,
among farms and families hard at work,
there lived a boy who loved trees.

Trees meant
shade,
food,
and shelter for many.

But each rainy season, floodwaters swallowed
more and more of the beautiful tree-covered land.
The boy's precious island was shrinking—
eroding away with the rushing river,
leaving empty sandbars behind.

The boy witnessed animals stranded on those sandbars,
their homes destroyed.
He feared that if animals withered without trees,
people would too.

The boy shared his fears with the village.
The elders explained that the only way to help animals
was to create new homes for them.
They gifted the boy with twenty bamboo saplings.

Alone, he canoed down the muddy river.
He wished he could cover all the land with trees …

but a large sandbar nearby was a place to start.
The land was too barren for animals,
the shores too sandy for leafy trees.
Would bamboo grow? The boy hoped.

Determined, he began to plant.
One shaft … two … then three.

Every day, he watered the saplings by hand,
sweat trickling down his face and chest.

He built a watering system to help …

and lugged heavy buckets from the river.
His arms grew tired, his back sore.

Still, each day, he tended to the plants.
And, over time, the bamboo patch grew …

… into a healthy thicket.
The boy was proud of his work,
but he worried it wouldn't be enough
to stop the swelling river or to provide shelter for animals.
If he wanted more plants to grow,
he would have to create a richer soil.

The boy carried cow dung, earthworms, termites, and angry red ants that bit him on the journey to their new home.

He brought seeds from neighboring villages,

over trails,

through brush,

down the river.

Each day, he planted.

As years passed and the boy grew, so did a forest.
Ten acres … twenty acres … then forty.

Wildlife returned for the first time in many years:

buffalo, one-horned rhinos, and snakes,
gibbons, migratory birds, and elephants.

The man's forest teemed with
life and diversity.

Not everyone was happy.

Fear swept over the villages when tigers arrived.

So the man planted more grasses to attract small animals

that would keep the tigers happy in the forest.

Elephants wandered into neighboring farms to feast on the crops.
So the man planted more fruiting trees to help feed the hungry elephants.

Some wanted to harvest the forest to build homes,
but the man was there to plant anew.

Others tried to hunt the animals for their horns and fur,
but the man was there to protect.

Few thought the forest would last,
but the man believed in its strength.

Now, in India,
on a large river island,
among wildlife and trees as tall as buildings,
there lives a man who has planted a forest.
The forest is called Molai, after a man named
Jadav "Molai" Payeng,
who never stopped planting and pruning and protecting.

"Only by growing plants, the Earth will survive."

–Jadav Payeng

Jadav "Molai" Payeng grew up near Majuli Island—one of the world's largest river islands—located in the Brahmaputra River, in northeastern India. As a young teenager, Jadav witnessed the death of hundreds of snakes that floodwaters stranded on a barren sandbar near the island. Heartbroken over the snakes, in 1979 Jadav began planting to help his beloved island and the wildlife who shared it with him.

Since then, defying all odds, Jadav has quietly planted, nurtured, and grown an entire forest on his own. Named after him, Molai Forest is said to be over 1,300 acres—that's larger than 900 football fields—and still growing! The forest is now home to thousands of different species of plants and trees. This unexpected sanctuary provides life and shelter for many animals, some endangered.

In 2008, almost thirty years after he planted his first seedlings, Jadav's forest was discovered by local authorities tracking a herd of elephants. Since then, Jadav has been recognized worldwide and received numerous awards and honors, including the title: "The Forest Man of India."

Jadav hopes his mission will inspire others to make the world a greener place. If one person can plant an entire forest, can you imagine what many could do?

Author's Note

Jadav's love of the Earth and his ideas on reforestation are important concepts that I also hold dear. I grew up in northern Florida, surrounded by forests. My father was a prominent forest ecologist, my mother was a science writer, and our house was constantly filled with visiting scientists from around the world. I especially enjoyed listening to their tales of the environment and faraway places. And, as I grew older, I developed a deep love for our planet and a keen interest in sharing its wonderful stories.

I hope that Jadav's story triggers your inner ecologist, as it did mine. If you plant a seed today, you never know what it might become, so plant on.

Plant a Forest of Your Own

⚹ ⟋ Seed Planting ⟍ ⚹

Whether you are planting trees, grass, fruits, or vegetables,
every time you plant a seed, you help make Earth a greener place.

Materials:

Paper towels, water, glass jar or clear cup, seeds

NOTE: Some faster-growing seeds include radishes, beans, peas, and a variety of flowers.

Directions:

1) Soak your paper towels in water and wring them out.

2) Layer your wet paper towels into your container. Dump out any extra water.

3) Push 3-4 seeds about halfway down between the side of the container and the paper towels.

4) Label the seeds. Use a permanent marker to write the name of the seed on the outside of the container, next to the seed.

5) Place your container in the sun. You will need to sprinkle water over your paper towels once a day as the seeds sprout and the plants grow.

6) After 7 to 14 days, your seeds will have sprouted and are ready for planting. Carefully transfer your sprouts either outside or to a pot with soil. If you are planting outside, choose an area where your type of plant will be happy. A good way to know where to plant is to check out local plant books from your library or ask an adult.

For my dad, who showed me how big of an impact a single person can make.
— S. G.

✦ ✦ ✦

For every small child with a big dream.
— K. H.

Text Copyright © 2019 Sophia M. Gholz
Illustration Copyright © 2019 Kayla Harren
Design Copyright © 2019 Sleeping Bear Press

Sleeping Bear Press™
2395 South Huron Parkway, Suite 200, Ann Arbor, MI 48104
www.sleepingbearpress.com
© Sleeping Bear Press

Library of Congress Cataloging-in-Publication Data
Names: Gholz, Sophia M., author. | Harren, Kayla, illustrator.
Title: The boy who grew a forest : the true story of Jadav Payeng / written
by Sophia M. Gholz ; illustrated by Kayla Harren.
Description: Ann Arbor, Michigan : Sleeping Bear Press, [2018] | Audience: Ages: 4-8.
Identifiers: LCCN 2018037506 | ISBN 9781534110243 (hardcover)
Subjects: LCSH: Pāẏeṅa, Ẏādawa, 1963---Juvenile literature. |
Environmentalists--India--Jorhāt (District)--Biography--Juvenile
literature. | Foresters--India--Jorhāt (District)--Biography--Juvenile literature.
Classification: LCC GE56.P39 G46 2018 | DDC 333.95/316092 [B] --dc23
LC record available at https://lccn.loc.gov/2018037506

Printed and bound in the United States
10 9 8